ROBERT QUACKENBUSH

THE MAN ON THE FLYING TRAPEZE

The Circus Life of Emmett Kelly, Sr., told with pictures & song!

J.B. LIPPINCOTT COMPANY · PHILADELPHIA AND NEW YORK

For Emmett Kelly, Sr.,
the father of modern American circus clowns,
with deepest thanks and appreciation
. . . and for Piet's sake!

U.S. Library of Congress Cataloging in Publication Data. Quackenbush, Robert M. The man on the flying trapeze: the circus life of Emmett Kelly, Sr., told with pictures & song! SUMMARY: The circus experiences of Emmett Kelly, Sr., "America's favorite clown," are related in verse to be sung to the tune of the familiar song "The Man on the Flying Trapeze." 1. Kelly, Emmett, 1898- —Juvenile literature. 2. Clowns—Juvenile literature. [1. Kelly, Emmett, 1898- 2. Clowns. 3. Circus. 4. Songs] I. Title. GV1811.K4Q32 791.3'3'0924 [92] 75-5614 ISBN-0-397-31643-7

A NOTE

Trapeze artists have been part of American circuses for over a hundred years. Their glittering costumes and gravity-defying feats of flight made them glamorous heroes of circus lore and inspired one of our earliest circus songs, "The Man on the Flying Trapeze." The verses have told many different stories, but the tune has always remained as it was played and sung in the nineteenth century.

In this book, the song tells the story of Emmett Kelly, Sr., who was a "man on the flying trapeze" until the Great Depression of 1929. Like a great many people in those difficult times, young Kelly had to take any work he could get in order to support his family. But although Kelly may have felt that the change from spangled tights to a clown's costume would be something of a comedown, Willie—the sad-faced, ragged figure he created—captured the hearts of all who saw him, and today clowns patterned after Willie can be seen in circuses all over this country.

Here, in his seventh picture–song book of Americana, Robert Quackenbush relates the circus experiences of Emmett Kelly, Sr.—to the tune of the familiar refrain, "The Man on the Flying Trapeze."

OH!   He flew through the air with the greatest of ease,
The daring young man on the flying trapeze.
Whene'er he appeared, the crowd he did please,
And ovations were given to him.

OH! He flew through the air like the wind in the trees,
The dashing young man on the flying trapeze.
He teamed with a girl; they flew with such ease,
Their "iron jaw" act was a hit.

OH! He married his partner, the girl on his swing;
They worked together, two hearts on the wing.
Their act was the best to be seen in the ring,
Till misfortune came into their lives.

OH!   Depression had all of our country upset,
      Money was scarcer, and work hard to get.
      Their circus shut down when it went into debt,
      And their "trap" act was out in the cold.

OH!   He'd flown through the air like a sail in the breeze,
This daring young man on the flying trapeze.
Now other shows closed, for they all felt the squeeze,
And his rigging lay gathering dust.

OH!   He tried to find work, but the tale was the same —
There was none to be found, in spite of his fame.
At last someone offered a job he could claim —
'Twas a single, without a trapeze.

OH!   The circus would give him the part of a clown.
      "I'll do it," he said. "I can't turn the job down.
      My family is hungry, there's no work in town."
      With that he accepted the pay.

OH!   "A clown with a sad face I think I will be,
Someone," he said, "who's a real part of me.
He'll be so sad and so mournful to see."
But would he make anyone laugh?

OH!   He'd flown through the air with such courage and ease,
The daring young man on the flying trapeze.
Now he put on his clown face while hoping to please
The people who'd given him work.

OH! The circus began with the clown so forlorn,
Dressed as a hobo, all tattered and torn.
As he started his antics, a new star was born,
For the crowd roared with laughter and cheered.

OH!　This young man's clown, after opening night,
Was the toast of the town and the children's delight.
His rags showed he shared in America's plight,
And the people found humor in him.

OH! "Willie" the clown became famous worldwide,
From Boston to 'Frisco, across the Divide.
Though royalty loved him, he took it in stride
And gave little children his best.

OH! He'd flown through the air like a leaf in the breeze,
The daring young man on the flying trapeze.
But his greatest fame came to him with such ease,
As America's favorite clown!

THE MAN ON THE FLYING TRAPEZE

OH! He flew through the air with the great-est of ease, The

dar—ing young man on the fly~ing trap~eze. When~

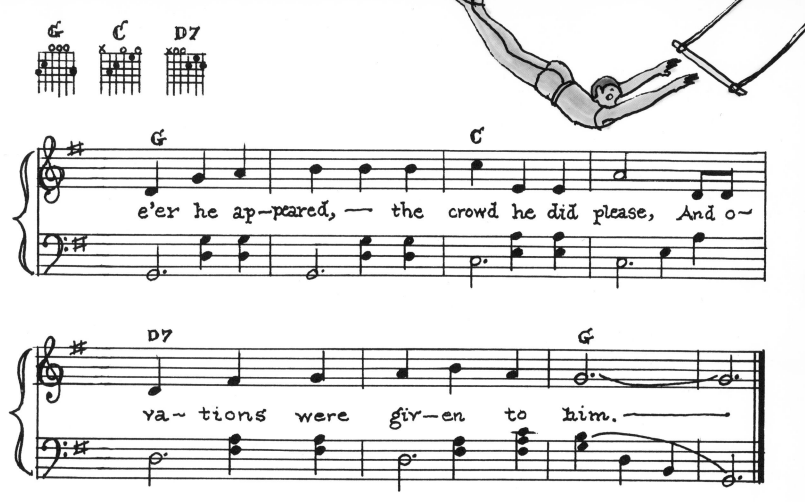

e'er he ap-peared, — the crowd he did please, And o-

va~ tions were giv-en to him. ———

arranged by Marguerite O. Daly

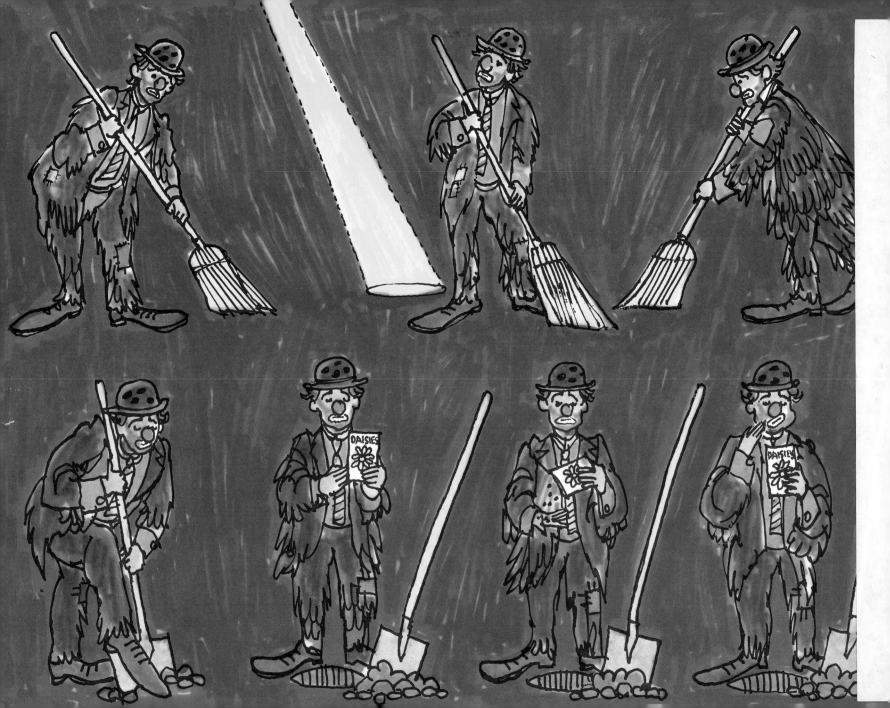